Pat Skene

Illustrated by Graham Ross

ORCA BOOK PUBLISHERS

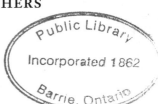

Library and Archives Canada Cataloguing in Publication

Skene, Pat, 1945-

What a hippopota-mess! / Pat Skene; illustrated by Graham Ross.

(Orca echoes)

ISBN 1-55143-402-4

1. Animals--Juvenile poetry. 2. Children's poetry, Canadian (English).

I. Ross, Graham, 1962- II. Title. III. Series.

PS8637.K454W43 2006   jC811'.6   C2006-902705-6

First Published in the United States: 2006
Library of Congress Control Number: 2006927096

Summary: Playful poems about animals are combined
with funny and informative interviews and lists of facts.

Orca Book Publishers gratefully acknowledges the support for its publishing programs
provided by the following agencies: the Government of Canada through the Book Publishing
Industry Development Program and the Canada Council for the Arts, and the Province of
British Columbia through the BC Arts Council and the Book Publishing Tax Credit.

Designed by Lynn O'Rourke
Typesetting by Doug McCaffry
Illustrations by Graham Ross

Orca Book Publishers
PO Box 5626, Stn. B
Victoria, BC Canada
V8R 6S4

Orca Book Publishers
PO Box 468
Custer, WA USA
98240-0468

www.orcabook.com
Printed and bound in Canada
Printed on recycled paper, 60% PCW.
09 08 07 06 • 4 3 2 1

For Farrell and her sparkling imagination.
—P.S.

For Olivia, our future singing star,
and the star that lights up my life.
—G.R.

Contents

What a Hippopota-Mess!

Now, if you're like a lot of us
and think a hippopotamus
would never make a lot of fuss,
well, then you would be wrong.

I saw two hippopotami
when they were peeking water-high.
One hippo seemed a friendly guy,
but not for very long!

He twitched his hippopota-ear
and started swimming very near.
He said, "Hey, Bud! Come over here!"
I tried to run away.

He chased me with his hippo-feet.
"Wait up!" he said. "My name is Pete!"
And then he dragged me by the seat
right back into the bay.

Pete swam the hippopota-stroke.
He held me in a hippo-choke.
I gave his meaty ribs a poke.
He made a grunting noise.

That's when Pete's hippopota-pal
said, "Hiya, Bud! My name is Sal.
I'm just a hungry hippo-gal.
And I eat little boys!"

She flicked her hippopota-tail
and saw my face was rather pale.
Sal's hippopota-breath was stale.
She licked me on the nose.

I said, "You're hippo-fooling me.
I know you don't eat meat, you see."
"You're right, dear boy," she said with glee.
"But I could eat your clothes!"

They grinned those hippopota-smiles.
Their hippo-laughs were heard for miles.
But then we spotted crocodiles.
They looked like floating logs.

Pete acted like a hippo-ham.
He honked and wheezed, but Sal yelled, "Scram!"
And then we kind of gallop-swam,
like hippo-jumping frogs.

I rode to shore on hippo-Pete.
The hippopota-ride was neat.
But I kept sliding off my seat,
just like a rodeo.

When we were safe on hippo-land,
their hippo-tears dropped in the sand.
They both said, "Bud, you understand.
We have nowhere to go."

I looked into Pete's hippo-eyes.
I listened to Sal's hippo-sighs.
And I said, "Hey, don't worry, guys,
I live right over there."

They hippopota'd to my room.
Pete said, "There's not much hippo-room."
And then I heard an awful BOOM!
Sal flattened out my chair.

All night, their four-toed hippo-feet
danced to the hippopota-beat.
I fed them everything but meat.
Their breath made such a stink!

They sloshed their hippopota-tea.
I hosed them down all night till three.
My room was a catastrophe!
I didn't sleep a wink.

Those hippos partied-on till dawn.
Oh, how I wished those guys were gone.
Pete threw my bed out on the lawn
to make room on the floor.

My tub was full of hippo-juice.
They always had a good excuse.
How could I set those hippos loose?
I hollered out, "NO MORE!"

I said, "You hippopotami
are bugging me. Now say good-bye!"
"We like it here," I heard them cry.
That's when I called the ZOO.

They jumped up with a hippo-thud.
Pete said, "So long. We'll see you, Bud.
We're off to roll in hippo-mud
and find a better view."

Now what a hippopota-mess!
My room was full of watercress.
They left a sweaty pinkish mess
on everything I own.

So if you see those hippo-guys,
don't look into their hippo-eyes.
They'll call you Bud, but if you're wise
you won't invite them home!

An Interview with Pete and Sal

1. How big are you?

Pete: I guess I'm about the size of an average car. But I weigh more than three cars put together. We hippos often have vicious fights with other creatures and with each other. We have big tusk-teeth too. It's no wonder we scared poor Bud.

2. What do hippos like to eat?

Sal: We're vegetarians and love to eat plants and grassy stuff. I eat about 300 pounds (140 kilograms) of food every day. That's almost 150 boxes of kids' cereal. But then it rots in my stomach and gives me bad breath. *Burp!*

3. How big is your mouth?

Pete: I have about forty big hippo-teeth. They're made of ivory, just like elephant tusks. I can open my mouth really wide. You could probably stand up in it!

4. Are you afraid of crocodiles?

Sal: No, we're much bigger than crocodiles. They know better than to bother us. But Pete and I were afraid they might eat Bud. We got out of there fast! We hippos gallop when we swim. Bud really liked riding on Pete's back, just like baby hippos do.

5. Why did you drag Bud into the water in the first place?

Pete: Oh, we were just hippo-ing around. Sal and I were having a boring day and looking for something to do. We liked Bud but hippos don't usually want humans to come near us. Hippopota-rumor has it that we're one of the most dangerous animals in Africa. I'm glad Bud met us on a good-mood day, aren't you?

6. What is the weirdest thing about hippos?

Sal: Well, one really cool thing is that our sweat is pinkish red. So sometimes it looks like we're sweating blood. We splashed a lot of sweat around Bud's room. It made everything look pink. I don't think Bud liked pink! He said his room was a real mess. A "catastrophe" he called it.

7. How long have hippos been around?

Pete: Would you believe over five million years? Well, not me personally. But did you know that crocodiles have outlived the dinosaurs? Crocodiles have been around for over seventy million years. They've hardly changed at all. They're so cranky!

8. Do hippos like being in the water all the time?

Sal: We sure do! Our eyes and ears are on the top of our heads. That way, we can stay under the water with just our eyes sticking out and still see everything. That's how Pete spotted Bud. We can also sink down and run underwater on the bottom of the river. Pretty neat, huh?

9. Why were you honking and wheezing when you saw the crocodiles?

Pete: I did that to scare them away. I can also grunt and bellow really loud. Sometimes I yawn a lot with my big hippo-mouth. That works to frighten everybody too.

10. What does "hippopotamus" mean?

Sal: It means "river horse." But then again, hippos are closely related to the pig family. Maybe we should be called "river pigs." And, oh yes, we're also related to camels and giraffes. So does that make us "river camels" or "river giraffes" too? Hmm.

Creepy-Crawl-Critters

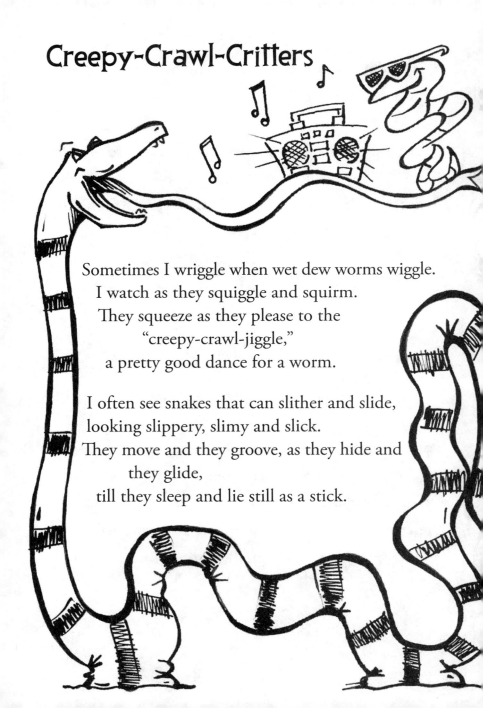

Sometimes I wriggle when wet dew worms wiggle.
I watch as they squiggle and squirm.
They squeeze as they please to the
"creepy-crawl-jiggle,"
a pretty good dance for a worm.

I often see snakes that can slither and slide,
looking slippery, slimy and slick.
They move and they groove, as they hide and
they glide,
till they sleep and lie still as a stick.

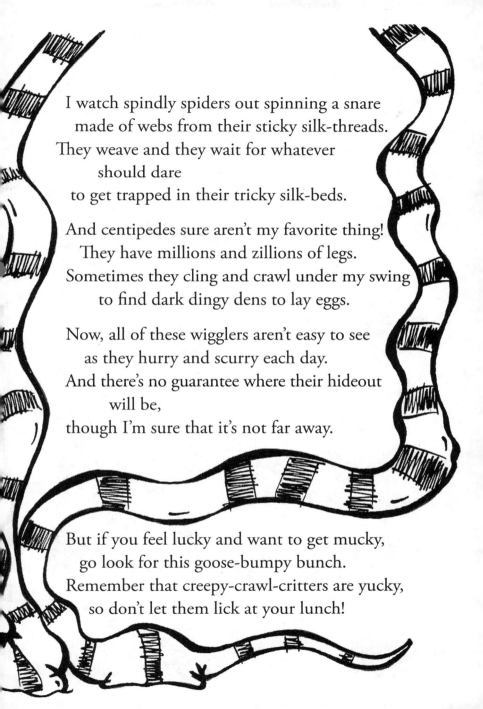

I watch spindly spiders out spinning a snare
    made of webs from their sticky silk-threads.
They weave and they wait for whatever
        should dare
    to get trapped in their tricky silk-beds.

And centipedes sure aren't my favorite thing!
    They have millions and zillions of legs.
Sometimes they cling and crawl under my swing
        to find dark dingy dens to lay eggs.

Now, all of these wigglers aren't easy to see
    as they hurry and scurry each day.
And there's no guarantee where their hideout
        will be,
    though I'm sure that it's not far away.

But if you feel lucky and want to get mucky,
    go look for this goose-bumpy bunch.
Remember that creepy-crawl-critters are yucky,
    so don't let them lick at your lunch!

Cool Critter Facts

1. Worms eat dirt.

Dew worms live for about six years. They have no eyes, and they breathe through their skin. Every day they eat up to one-third of their body weight. Earthworms have no teeth. They swallow the soil as they burrow into it. Dirt is good for them. What a way to get your vitamins!

2. Snakes have BIG mouths.

Snakes have a narrow body, a small head and no teeth. Yet they swallow their prey whole! (It would be like you trying to swallow a watermelon.) Snakes can do this because their skin is elastic and their jaws are loosely joined. They dislocate and expand their jaws to swallow big things. Did you know that there are no snakes in Newfoundland, Ireland or New Zealand?

3.   Spiders can sew.

All spiders spin silk. Spider silk is made inside their bodies. Only some spiders spin webs. All spiders spin sticky threads called "draglines." They send out a thread that floats in the air until it sticks to something. Just like Spiderman! They use draglines to jump, drop or swing safely away from enemies. Spider silk is the strongest natural fiber in the world.

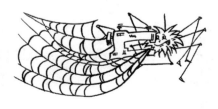

4. Centipedes and lobsters are cousins.

The name "centipede" means one hundred feet. Not all centipedes have that many. But some have even more, depending on the species. When one of their legs is cut off, it grows back. Centipedes aren't insects. They're related to the lobster family.

Riddle: What goes "ninety-nine—
    clunk—ninety-nine—clunk?"
Answer: A centipede with a
    wooden leg.

More creepy-cool stuff: Spider blood is bluish in color. A snake's eyes turn blue as it gets ready to shed its skin. Snake skin isn't slippery and slimy at all, but dry. A rattlesnake can't hear the sound of its own rattles. Centipedes are blind, and some of them glow in the dark. And all earthworms are both male and female at the same time.

Smiling Jack

One sunny day, a lizard by the name of Smiling Jack
    stood looking in the water at a lizard looking back.
He asked his friend the otter. He said, "Ott, what
    should I do?"
The otter said, "I gotta see who's looking back at you."

So Ott looked in the water. Then the otter said, "I see...
    not a lizard, but an otter. He's looking back at me!"
The lizard and the otter went to see their friend the frog.
He was leaping on the lily pads around the foggy bog.

"Hey, Croak!" called out the lizard. "Could we have some
    of your time?

Is someone down there looking back below the
    waterline?"
The frog said, "I can take a look to see what I can see.
But we could look together. You could all look in
    with me."

They leaned toward the water for a better look close-up.
Three noses nearly touched three other noses
    pointing up.
Six goggled eyes looked quite surprised when six eyes
    goggled back!
They stared at Ott the otter, Croak the frog and
    Smiling Jack.

The otter said, "Who can they be? They are a handsome
    bunch.
They might be here to scare us. Do you think they want
    our lunch?"
And Jack said, "Maybe there's a way to put our minds to rest.

We'll find out if they're friend or foe. Let's put them to
  a test."

"Yes, we otta!" cried the otter. The frog croaked,
  "I agree.
Let's wave and smile and show them we're as friendly as
  can be."
And so they did and so it was...that all of them
  waved back.
"Good day!" cried Ott the otter, Croak the frog and
  Smiling Jack.

Then Ott said, "Well, I'm diving in. I want to say hello.
They're waving up. We're waving down. So let's all go
  below."
And Jack said, "Let's jump on their heads!" He grinned
  that lizard grin.
Splash went the frog into the bog, and all of them
  leaped in.

Now deep beneath the water they began to check around.
They listened for those strangers, but they never heard a
  sound.
The otter held his breath so long that he was turning blue.
He gurgled through the bubbles, "Let's keep looking for
  a clue."

They peeked beneath the lily pads and looked behind
  the reeds.
And Croak said, "I can see them hiding in that clump
  of weeds."

But it was only Callie and her catfish friends at play.
And when they saw that bug-eyed frog, those mud cats
   swam away.

"Where can they be?" the otter said. "There's nowhere
   left to look.
I've even talked to Archibald in Snapping-Turtle Nook.
He said to ask the pitcher plants, but they were catching food.
They wouldn't say one word to me. Those hairy plants
   are rude!"

"They're rude all right," said Smiling Jack. "On that we
   all agree.
Now where do you suppose that those three smiling
   guys could be?"
"Oh no!" cried Ott the otter. "Do you think they stole
   our lunch?
I always thought the three of them looked like a
   slippery bunch."

But all their snacks were safe and looked delicious like
before.

And then the sky grew dark as night, and rain began to
pour.

While thunder crashed, the lightning flashed. It put on
quite a show.

"I wonder," said the otter, "if they're watching from below."

"Let's tiptoe to the water," said the frog. "They could be
there."

Their goggled eyes stared in the pond while rain splashed
everywhere.

Then Smiling Jack said, "It's the storm that scared those
three away.

They've disappeared, but maybe they'll come back some
sunny day."

So that's the way they left it, and they went and ate
their lunch.

31

They talked about the weather and about that handsome
bunch.

They told the tale to all their friends, "Six goggled eyes
looked back!"

What a day for Ott the otter, Croak the frog and
Smiling Jack.

An Interview with the Lizard, Smiling Jack

1. How did you get a name like Smiling Jack?

Smiling Jack: Look at my face and you'll know the answer. I have always smiled a lot because it makes me feel good. I was born this way.

2. What kind of lizard are you?

Smiling Jack: I'm called a gecko, but there are 2500 different kinds of lizards. Some can even squirt blood from their eyes. These are called horned lizards. Frilled lizards have big funny collars around their necks. The basilisk lizard can run on top of water.

3. What's a pitcher plant?

Smiling Jack: These are really cool carnivorous plants—that means they eat meat. They like to live in marshy places and eat bugs, like water insects and mosquito eggs. They catch them with their hairy jaws and squeeze the juice right out of them. Yummy!

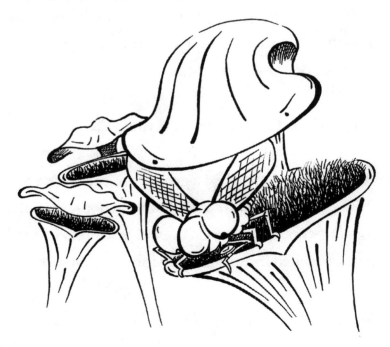

4.   What do frogs eat?

Smiling Jack: Frogs like bugs and worms mostly. Some bullfrogs can catch and eat a bat. Frogs swallow their food whole. They absorb water through their skin, so they don't have to drink. Pretty cool.

5.   What does Ott the otter like to do?

Smiling Jack: Otters are very smart and really know how to have fun. Ott likes to slide headfirst on his stomach down a muddy hill. He does it over and over. Did you know that otters are in the skunk family?

6.   Why did Ott the otter turn blue?

Smiling Jack: Otters love to do somersaults and acrobatics underwater. They can hold their breath for up to four minutes. (But they don't really turn blue doing it!) They also like to wrestle with each other and do belly flops into the water.

7.   What is the weirdest thing you've ever seen in the pond?

Smiling Jack: There are lots of strange critters in the pond. Frogs have got to be the weirdest. When they eat something that isn't good for them, some frogs can throw up their whole stomach. (The stomach stays attached and hangs out of their mouth.) Then the frog cleans it with a front leg and swallows it back down again. Yuck!

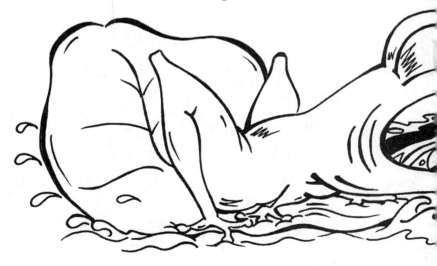

8. Do you ever think you'll see those three guys in the water again?

Smiling Jack: Oh, I'm sure of it. One of them was down there the other day when I looked in. It was the lizard and he was alone. He might be shy, so I think he'll come back on a sunny day with his friends to say hello.

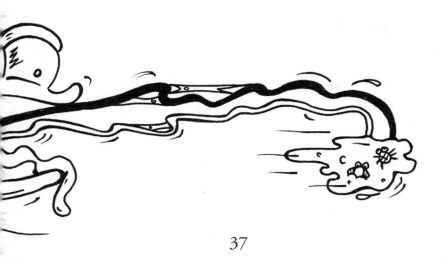

My Sleeping Tree

When early April showers sing,
they wake my cherry tree in spring.

Red robins cry their cheery song
while baby buds are growing strong.

Soft velvet flowers burst in bloom,
then fade away some time in June.

Warm rustling leaves in late July
send summer whispers to the sky.

But soon October sounds the bell
to signal fall's enchanting spell.

Now autumn flutters through the air
and dances till my tree is bare.

As sure as robins leave the nest,
a fading sun means time to rest.

When north winds of December blow,
my tree stands dreaming in the snow.

Cold winter branches dusted white
sway softly in the moonlit night.

But nature's magic gift goes on
and feeds the seasons, dusk to dawn.

So once again, my sleeping tree
will wait for spring to set it free.

Treevia for Kids

1. Trees aren't elephants.

But trees are plants with big trunks. They also have roots that anchor them in the ground. Tree roots suck up minerals and water from the earth. Some trees have needles and cones instead of leaves.

2. Start counting.

There are over 20,000 different kinds of trees. Of course, that doesn't include all the shoe trees, family trees and hat trees.

3. Plant a tree and breathe.

Trees are the air conditioners of the world. They breathe in carbon dioxide and breathe out oxygen we need to live. Two mature trees can provide enough oxygen for a family of four.

4. Tables, tires and teeth.

Trees are used to make furniture and build houses. They are also grown for their delicious fruits and nuts. Different tree parts can be found in tires, paint, cereal, chewing gum, hair spray, toothpaste and mouthwash.

5. O Canada!

The beautiful and fiery maple tree is the national tree of Canada. Check out the red maple leaf on the Canadian flag too.

6. Different leaves for different trees.

Most "deciduous" trees (like the cherry tree in this poem) shed their leaves every fall. "Evergreen" trees (like pine and spruce) drop and replace their leaves and needles too. But they do it only a few at a time all year long. That's why they stay "ever green."

7. Look out below!

Did you know that oak trees get struck by lightning more often than other trees? It's because they grow taller and make an easier target.

8. It isn't easy being green.

The leaves on deciduous trees need lots of sun to stay green. In the fall, the days get shorter and there is less sunlight. That's why the leaves turn yellow and brown and fall off the trees.

9. Trees can hibernate too.

Trees go through five stages in each cycle—they start, bud, grow, store food and rest (or sleep). Then, when the "sleeping trees" wake up, they start the cycle all over again.

10. What stories they could tell.

Trees are the oldest and biggest living organisms on Earth. Don't you wish they could talk and tell you stories about dinosaurs? Or maybe tales of knights in shining armor? What questions would you ask an ancient tree?

Blue Muckles Brown

Away up in the cold white north,
nearby a Yukon town,
there was a moose out on the loose
they called Blue Muckles Brown.

Folks recognized him right away
because his hide was blue.
His antlers drooped with clumps of ice.
He shivered all day through.

Now, moose lore spread for miles around
about this blue-moose sight.

And tales were told how he was brown,
but changed to blue one night.

They say it happened when the land
was gripped by bitter frost.
When piercing purple skies grew dark,
poor Muckles—he got lost.

He drifted through sub-zero cold
and roamed all afternoon.
He fell asleep right there beneath
the blue face of the moon.

He dreamed of playing hide-moose-seek
with sheep and caribou.
He snored as northern lights streaked by
and disappeared from view.

Then how those arctic winds did howl,
and how the snow did blow.

And how the ice did blanket him
that night so long ago.

When morning came and Muckles woke,
the land was white and still.
And overnight he'd changed all right.
He'd turned blue from the chill!

Through many wintry moons he shook
and shivered to the bone.
He dreamed that someday he'd be warm,
but stayed as cold as stone.

One chilly Yukon afternoon,
his moose-chores were all done.
Some friends cheered, "It's hoof-hockey time!
Hey, Muckles, join the fun!"

But Muckles shook his ice-clogged rack
and grunted now and then.
His moose-teeth chattered as he vowed,
"I won't be cold again!"

He watched the curling chimney smoke
rise from the village roofs.
He stomped his big moose-feet to leave
with snow caked on his hoofs.

Determined as a moose could be,
Blue Muckles Brown turned east.
He trotted toward the Yukon town
that beckoned this cold beast.

The children welcomed him with food
(smoked smelly-fish and ham).
And when this blue moose wouldn't eat,
they brought crowberry jam.

Then Muckles said, "You're all so nice,
and please don't think I'm bold.
But I'd much rather have some clothes.
You see…I'm rather cold."

They searched their closets and their drawers
for stuff a moose could wear.
They gathered all the fluffy wools
and warm things they could spare.

Despite the way they tugged and stretched,
it mattered not one bit.
The village kids had to agree—
this moose was hard to fit!

Their mukluks were too minuscule.
Their sweaters were too small.
Their parkas looked peculiar.
Their wool socks made him fall.

Then someone said, "Take him inside.
It's heat he's looking for."
But Muckles' antlers were too wide
to push him through the door.

"We're sorry, Muckles," cried the kids,
"but we can't seem to win.
We wish that we could help you out.
A cold front's moving in."

Now just the thought of being chilled
made Muckles jump for heat.
His moose-hoofs clacked so fast and hard
that sparks flew from his feet.

"I'm thawing out," Muckles exclaimed.
"I'm feeling warm as toast.
So now whenever I feel cold,
I'll dance until I roast!"

The harder Muckles did that jig,
the hotter those sparks got.
And soon the ground around his feet
was smoldering red-hot.

His blue moose-coat was turning brown.
His antlers soon caught fire.
His ears were smudged with soot and smoke.
But he danced even higher.

The children squealed as pumper-trucks
honk-honked their way through town.
Soon firefighters rushed to help
and hosed poor Muckles down.

They said, "That crazy jig you do
has caused these sparks to fly.
Next time you dance to warm yourself,
just call and we'll stand by."

Now Muckles doesn't hate the cold.
He loves a Yukon storm.
He dances the Moose-Muckle-Jig
until he's toasty warm.

But firefighters stay on-call
in moose-alert attire.
They'll race cross-town to splash him down
if Muckles catches fire!

An Interview with Blue Muckles Brown

1. What kind of name is Muckles?

Muckles: The word "muckle" means "a large amount." Since I'm a very big moose, it's a good name for me, don't you think?

2. How big are you?

Muckles: The biggest moose in the world live in the Yukon and Alaska. If I raise my head up, I could probably touch the ceiling in your house with my antlers. I weigh more than six refrigerators!

3. Why wouldn't you eat the food that the kids gave you?

Muckles: Because moose are vegetarians. We only like to eat twigs, shrubs and plants. I eat about forty-five pounds (twenty kilograms) of food every day. That's like twenty boxes of kids' cereal.

4. Could you get warm by standing in the sun?

Muckles: In the Yukon, we only have about four hours of daylight in the winter months. There are days in December when the sun never comes up at all. But I like June the best because sometimes the sun stays out all night.

5. Are there any birds in the Yukon?

Muckles: The big black raven is the official bird of the Yukon. It's known as the "trickster" because it can imitate noises like a barking dog or brakes on a big truck. Ravens are very smart birds. They can even unlock your lunch box with their sharp beaks and eat your sandwich!

6. What do northern lights look like?

Muckles: The northern lights (also called aurora borealis) are streamers of beautiful colors. They move across the sky at night like shimmering rainbows.

7. What are mukluks?

Muckles: They're warm winter boots decorated with fur trim and beads. People wear them to keep their feet warm. I sure could use a pair of those!

Dandelion Wishes

"Those dandelions are noxious weeds!"
I've heard some people say.
"Let's dig them out and mow them down.
Let's make them go away."

But dandelions are friends of mine.
I'd save them if I could.
I think they're just mischievous
and so misunderstood.

I see them sprout like polka dots
when spring starts to unfold.
Like ragamuffins in the sun,
their heads are spiked with gold.

I string them all together
in a necklace for my mom.
I pick some for my sister too.
They cheer her when she's glum.

And when like magic they grow tall,
my dandelions do tricks.
Their yellow heads turn fluffy white,
like cotton-balls on sticks.

That's when I make my secret wish
no one can overhear.
I gently blow the feathered puffs,
and *POOF*…they disappear!

Then all that's left are milky stems
out dancing in the breeze.
They peek at me from grassy fields.
I think they like to tease.

So dandelions are friends of mine.
They're not obnoxious weeds.
I know I'll see them all next year
because they left their seeds!

More Dandy Lines

1. What's in a name?

Dandelion leaves are saw-shaped, like jagged teeth. The name "dandelion" comes from the French words "dent-de-lion" or "lion's tooth." But in some places dandelions are also known as "swine's snout" (pig's nose). This is because of the way the flower looks when it's all closed up. Hmmm. Lion and swine and dandelion—they all rhyme too!

2. Digging makes more.

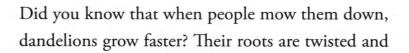

Did you know that when people mow them down, dandelions grow faster? Their roots are twisted and break up easily. So when people poke at them or try to dig them out, they're really making more roots. And more dandelions. What a trick that is!

3. Seeds with parachutes?

It's like magic when their sunny yellow flower-heads turn into fluffy white seed-balls. Each dandelion seed has a tiny parachute to help make it fly far and wide. That's how they spread everywhere. Dandelions love sunny places and are found all around the world. Imagine that!

4. Good to eat too.

Try collecting dandelions in the spring before they get too big and bitter. You can eat the leaves in salads, soups and sandwiches. Some people make dandelion jelly, pickles and even hair rinse with the yellow flowers. Dandelions must be really good to eat because over one hundred different insects like them too. Yummy!

5.   Not so yummy!

Even though you may love dandelions, not everyone does. Many people still use poisonous chemical sprays to stop them from spreading. So if chemicals are used where you live, please don't eat the dandelions! Yuk. But you can still blow away the feathery puffs and make dandelion wishes any time.

Pat Skene has eleven rocking chairs, including the one that her father gave her when she was two years old. She says that she does her best thinking when she is rocking back and forth. In fact, she wrote the first draft of *What a Hippopota-Mess!* during twenty minutes of rocking one night before dinner. Pat was a banker for many years. She loves her new life as a writer of rhymes. Pat lives in Cobourg, Ontario, with her husband.